The Tomato

by Texas Agricultural Experiment Station

with an introduction by Roger Chambers

Introduction

I am pleased to present yet another title on Gardening.

This volume is entitled "The Tomato" and was published in 1903.

The work is in the Public Domain and is re-printed here in accordance with Federal Laws.

As with all reprinted books of this age that are intended to perfectly reproduce the original edition, considerable pains and effort had to be undertaken to correct fading and sometimes outright damage to existing proofs of this title. At times, this task is quite monumental, requiring an almost total "rebuilding" of some pages from digital proofs of multiple copies. Despite this, imperfections still sometimes exist in the final proof and may detract from the visual appearance of the text.

I hope you enjoy reading this book as much as I enjoyed making it available to readers again.

Roger Chambers

CONTENTS.

EARLY TOMATOES.

On account of recent notable successes made by the East Texas growers, large numbers of our farmers are planting truck this season for the first time, and the demand on this department for information concerning the growing of garden products has been very great. The early tomato appears to be of most interest to the prospective truck farmer, and to supply him with practical information on this subject, is the object of the present bulletin. The contents are for the most part compilations from United States Experiment Station reports and other sources, and notes on the methods of our best Texas growers.

The successful production of an early tomato crop is more difficult than the production of any other truck crop commonly raised in Texas. While on some soils and under peculiarly favorable conditions the plants grow well and produce abundantly with little care, as a rule the tomato requires more skill and nicer management than any other crop. Owing to the remarkable profits obtained in some instances, the tomato is looked upon with special favor by those just starting into commercial trucking. It is advisable to make haste slowly with this crop. Obtain all of the information possible before starting and, for the first year, while gaining the experience so essential to full success, expend on the tomato plantation only that amount which you can lose without serious material injury to yourself. From the planting of the seed in the hot bed till the fruit is marketed the grower is beset by difficulties and problems which require for their solution careful thought, intelligent action and experience. After a year's experience with the tomato one becomes acquainted with its needs and its enemies, and is then ready to venture into raising the crop commercially with a measure of assurance of success.

SEED.

With a crop where so much depends upon earliness, and where it is so essentially important that from the planting of the seed forward no delay should occur, it is highly important that the seed be carefully chosen and thoroughly tested before time for starting the crop in the hot bed. It occasionally happens that seeds fail to grow and where the testing for vitality has been neglected a week or ten days are lost before their worthlessness is discovered in the hot bed. Add to this the length of time necessary to send for new seed from another firm and one gets an idea of the importance of a preliminary seed test. Avoid cheap seed and irresponsible firms, as the genuineness and quality of the seed are all-important. Obtain the seed early and test at once for vitality. This may be done in a manner satisfactory for all practical purposes with an apparatus consisting of two ordinary soup plates and a piece of undyed wool or flannel cloth.

Moisture, warmth, air and darkness are the essential conditions for the test. Thoroughly dampen the cloth with soft water, the

FIG. I.
Germinating Apparatus.
After A. J. Pieters, Div. Botany, U. S. Dept. of Agri. Year Book, 1895.

temperature of which should be 80° F. By actual count put two hundred seeds on one end of the cloth and fold the other end over onto them. Place the folded cloth flat on the bottom of one plate and invert the other over it. Set the tester in the ordinary living room and the temperature will be about right. Examine the seeds daily, picking out and keeping count of them as they germinate. This test may be supplemented by planting exactly two hundred seeds in a box of soil and placing same in a warm place until vegetation takes place. This is not as accurate a test as the former, but serves as a check. Tomatoes require eight to eleven days from seed to vegetation. Unless one hundred and eighty of the two hundred seeds germinate, the seed is not of good vitality; and in case the number is much less it will pay to change seedsmen. It is a practice among certain class of seedsmen to mix the left-over seed of one year with the new season's crop. The result is a mixture containing 25 to 50 per cent. of worthless material. The seed tester indicates the honest seedsman.

The subject of each grower selecting and saving his own seed is worthy of consideration by those who wish to be certain of the variety planted and who are striving to produce an extra-early improved type. The tomato responds quickly to selection and care, and this tendency will produce valuable results in a few seasons. In some instances, at least, the commercial tomato seed grower markets his best fruit and uses the small, late and green tomatoes for his contract with the seed house. Such seeds are of low vitality and the plants from them tend to inferior quality and later maturity. Furthermore, the seed grower may not have the variety isolated, in which case his product may prove a cross-bred tomato, more likely to be inferior than to be improved in any way. If each grower saves his own seed he can control all of the conditions, produce the earliest uniform crop of smooth fruit, improve his stock, and be certain of genuineness and purity.

There is some evidence that seed from the first ripe fruits do not tend to produce earlier tomatoes the following season, and information on this point is herewith presented for the growers' consideration. The following is from bulletin No. 70 of the Michigan Agricultural Experiment Station. "For three years we have attempted to learn the effects of planting seeds from the first fruits that ripened as compared with those selected late in the season. The first two years a slight gain in earliness of the crop was noticed, but it was observed that while this gain was considerable in the case of varieties of angular type, it became a loss when the smooth, apple-shaped sorts were considered." The third year the average of fifteen varieties was 143¾ days from seed to maturity and 145¾ days for the main crop, but as in the case of the previous years the smooth sorts showed a loss in earliness. The following is quoted from Cornell bulletin No. 45: "The poorest results were got from the seeds of the earliest fruits." There was no difference in the date of the first picking. "In our experiments last year there was no constant difference between the sets in point of earliness. This, illustrates the law that any fruit reproduces its parent rather than itself; that is, the character of the plant as a whole is more important than the character of any individual fruit upon it. We should, therefore, expect better results by selecting fruits from an early plant rather than by selecting early fruits from an ordinary plant."

It becomes evident from the above that it will not pay to select merely the early fruits, but that the selection must be of early plants. Choose vigorous plants which promise an early even crop of good fruit and mark them. It is not necessary nor desirable to take for seed the earliest ripe fruits. Let them go to market while the price is high, and use the later fruit from the marked plants.

A great deal has been done in an experimental way in producing earlier fruiting by using immature tomatoes for seed. In a majority of instances the seed from green tomatoes produced an earlier crop, but the fruit was inferior in keeping quality and the plants were weak and subject to disease.

The method of saving seed is simple, though it involves some disagreeable labor. The tomatoes are thrown into a barrel, crushed with a masher and left standing in a warm place until thoroughly fermented. The contents of the barrel are then washed through a coarse sieve, such as plasterers use in straining putty. This allows the seeds to pass through with the water, leaving skins and coarse material behind. A finer sieve separates the seed from the water as it passes from the coarse screen, and additional water is used to further wash the seed. When clean it is spread on cotton sheets and exposed to the sun to dry. Stir about frequently and protect from rain or high wind.

VARIETIES.

The question of varieties has been settled as far as the Texas grower is concerned. The Acme and Livingston Beauty are the asknowledged favorites. The Acme has proven most satisfactory in the tests at this station, but it has a tender skin and cracks badly in rainy weather. It is hoped that breeding and selection may develop a still more satisfactory variety than either of the above. At present the Acme and the Beauty are our best commercial tomatoes for the early market, and the following discussion concerns these varieties especially:

HOT BEDS.

In selecting a place for the hot bed, care should be taken to obtain a well drained piece of soil that is protected somewhat from the north wind. In this section good drainage is even more essential than protection from cold winds, but the best results are obtained where both features are provided for. A southern exposure is desirable, and the south side of an old rock fence forms an ideal location.

As soon as the location is decided upon, an excavation should be made, 26 to 30 inches deep, 6 feet wide, and the desired length. A frame 6 by 12 is sufficient to start enough plants for two acres. Drive four posts down in each corner and line the inside of the bed with 1x12 boards. The sides of the bed are then braced by 2x4's placed across every 3 feet of the frame. The frame work on the northern side of the bed should extend about 6 inches above

FIG. II.

Hot bed in center level with ground. Hot bed at right—old style. Glass and cotton sash.

the level of the ground, while that on the south side should not
come above the surface. This will give the sash sufficient pitch
to easily shed water and also to catch the rays of the sun in the
best possible manner. The earth should be banked up on the north
side until on a level with the top plank. A 1x6 board should now
be laid all around the bed to prevent the water from passing down
the sides of the frame, and to otherwise aid in its protection. 'Fig.
II gives an illustration of such a hot bed now in use at College.

A large majority of the hot beds are built with a considerable
portion of their framework above ground. A frame of this sort
is shown in Fig. III b.

Such a structure no doubt lessens the labor of excavation, but it
exposes the bed a great deal more to the cold winds, rendering the
temperature more variable and, consequently, increasing the danger of the plants being injured by a sudden freeze.

SASH.

There are two kinds in general use, the glass sash and the
cotton. The glass sash is the more expensive, but on account of
better service and durability, it is probably the more economical in
the long run. Glass sash can be made by a carpenter or bought
of our home lumber yards for $2.00 to $2.50 each. The cloth sash
is a 3x6 foot frame made of 1x3 inch stuff over which a piece of
domestic is tacked. The cloth is then given a thorough coating of
linseed oil. These sash or "cottons," as they are generally called,
should not cost over 25 cents each, and, if well cared for, they
will last from two to three years. Such cottons may be seen illus-
trated in Fig. 2. During severe cold weather the cottons are not
a sufficient covering, hence some form of matting should be provided. The common cotton bagging is probably the most convenient and economical for this purpose. Fig. 3 is an illustration of
double rows of hot beds on which continuous rolls of 8 oz. duck
canvas are used. When a covering is not needed the cloth is rolled
to the back of the bed.

COLD FRAMES.

The cold frame is constructed in essentially the same way as the
hot bed. The excavation, however, need not be so deep as there is
no heating material to be used beneath the soil. The cold frame
is seldom intended for permanent use, and, consequently, need not
be built of as durable material as the hot bed. Indeed, a loose,
temporary construction is desirable, as that allows its being taken
up and stored at the end of the season. The most economical sash
for the cold frame are the cottons, or 8 oz. canvas rolls as shown
in Fig. III, a, which are sufficient covering except in unusually
cool nights, when matting should be placed over them.

a

b

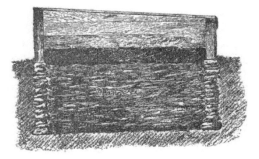

c

FIG. III.

After Bailey, Princ. of Veg. Growing.

a   Cold frame with canvas roll covering.
b   Raised hot bed.
c   Cross section of manure hot bed.

FLUE HOT BEDS.

There are some objections to manure or cotton-hull forcing beds, for example, the heat is not under control and may become rather too intense for a period, and subsequently become exhausted before the season is far enough advanced. Again, if the bed happens to become too heavily watered by accident or mismanagement, the plants may suffer from cold before the bottom heat again brings up the proper temperature. To obviate these difficulties many of our large growers are using the flue hot bed. This is made in the following manner: Lay off a trench six feet wide and as long as necessary to supply the number of plants needed. The maximum length of the bed, however, should be 60 feet. The trench should be 18 inches deep at the end farthest from the furnace and continue at a slight decline to within 8 feet of the throat of the fire-box, when it should dip at such an angle that it will reach the end of the bed about three feet from the surface. Along the floor of this bed two lines of flues should be laid. Each of these flues is made by placing two rows of bricks parallel to each other and at such a distance apart that the top may be closed by the laying of brick across them. This makes a flue of about 6x8 inches, inside measurement. The bricks are held to their place by mortar. At the furnace end of the bed a large pit should be arranged in which to build the brick arch and the fire-box. The arch should be large enough to take in chunks of rough wood, thus enabling one to have a cheap fuel supply and to maintain a steady fire through the night without special watching. At the end of the flues two upright chimneys should be made sufficiently high to cause the necessary draft through the flues. The chimney should be provided with dampers so that the draft can be shut off in case the heat becomes too great at any time. The bed may be made either of solid earth or upon a board foundation. The latter, while more costly, is the more satisfactory, as it allows a more even distribution of heat beneath the bed. If the solid bed is desired, it is simply necessary to throw in sufficient soil to cover the flues and level the bed to within 8 or 10 inches of the surface. In case a board foundation is needed, it will be necessary to put up a structure of 2x4's, making the frame about the inside of the bed and using inch boards for flooring. This floor should be level as in the case of the earth bed and the same distance below the surface of the ground. From this point forward the same directions for forming the seed bed apply as those given where manure is used as the source of heat. The frame and sash should be built in a manner similar to that advised for the other form of hot bed. Beside the absolute control of heat, there are several points in favor of the flue hot bed especially where sub-irrigation is employed in connection with it. For example, if the air becomes too warm, cold water may be put into the sub-irrigating tile, which will tend to cool them and the soil. The tile act as ventilators in case of excessive warmth, and also aerate the soil.

PREPARATION AND SOILS.

About the first of January the manure for the hot bed should be in readiness. Fresh horse droppings with an equal weight of straw litter or forest leaves are the best, and at the same time the most economical material that can be used. There are some people who advocate the use of cotton seed and hulls simply because nearly every farmer has more or less of them. When we realize, however, that cotton seed is worth from $15.00 to $20.00 per ton and hulls from $3.00 to $7.00, while manure may be had at almost every livery stable in the State at not more than 50 cents per ton, we can readily see the financial error that is made in the use of both cotton seed and hulls, especially when it is known that horse manure will give the best results. The manure should be placed in piles at first, and, if dry, it should be dampened thoroughly. A violent fermentation occurs, and if the bed is not turned every few days the manure is liable to "fire" and become severely injured. After the material has been turned two or three times, it is ready to be placed in the hot bed. The manure should be spread in the bed and thoroughly tramped until a depth of 15 to 20 inches is reached. A rich, sandy, loamy soil should then be added to a depth of 4 to 6 inches. Soil that has washed from a field into an old tank makes ideal material. If any vegetable matter is added, care should be taken to have it well rotted and thoroughly mixed with the soil. If too much is used, it furnishes a breeding place for the "damping off" germs and causes the soil to become sour. With such conditions very little success may be expected. A thin coating of air slaked lime, sulphur and tobacco dust should be spread over the surface and worked in to a depth of an inch. This has a very beneficial effect in reducing the ravages of fungus pests and aiding the young plants to a healthy, vigorous growth. Three or four days after the bed has been finished everything should be ready for sowing the seed. The temperature by this time, as told by a thermometer thrust through the soil into the heating material, should not register over 90° nor under 80°.

PLANTING.

Mark off rows across the bed 4 inches apart and not over half an inch deep. If seed has shown 90 per cent. germination, plant about four seeds to the inch; if seed is under 90 per cent., plant thicker correspondingly. The temperature of the bed should be held at from 65° to 70° F. at night and as near 80° as possible in the daytime. Ample ventilation must be allowed. The plants should appear in from eight to ten days under these conditions, and the bed should be so managed that from their appearance until transplanted to cold frames or pots the surface should never be *wet*. If possible keep the surface quite dry, supplying water from beneath by means of sub-irrigation. When the plants are up the temperature may be lowered to between 70° and 80° in daytime

FIG. VII.
Pot Grown Plant.
After Beach, N. Y. Exp. Sta. Bul. 125.

and from 60° to 70° at night. At all times guard against sudden changes toward unusual cold, for the tomato is a plant which delights in a warm, genial climate and a check from cold will hold it at a standstill for several days. Allow ventilation whenever possible, as fresh air is not only desirable, but essential.

The object from now forward is to produce strong, free-growing, stocky plants, ready for the field as soon as conditions are favorable. To do this they must have ample room at all times, hence in about thirty days from vegetation it will be found necessary to transplant and allow more space. The general practice among our growers is to move the plants to a cold frame at this time, which practice has proven very satisfactory. However, in Maryland transplanting to pots has given so much better results than the old method, that it is thought desirable to present the experience of the Maryland grower for consideration.

In growing tomatoes, as in any specialized business, those methods are sought which reduce labor expenditure, provided the method does not involve a prohibitive outlay on equipment. The use of pots from the seed bed forward reduces labor considerably, and does more in that it produces a finer and healthier plant than can be obtained in any other way. The potted plants when transplanted to the field experience no shock, but grow off at once, producing ripe fruit before those set from cold frames. With pots there is no "damping off," and there are no "leggy" plants, while with beds these evils are difficult to avoid.

In 1890 and 1891 experiments at Maryland station (see Bulletin No. 11) showed that potted plants produced earlier fruit and a much greater yield than cold frame plants. The Acme potted produced at the rate of 16.43 tons per acre as against 9.30 tons per acre of the bed plants. In 1891 an average yield of fifteen varieties was, for potted plants 18 tons per acre, and for cold frame plants 14½ tons. Besides the increased bulk, a larger crop of early fruit was grown from the potted plants.

As above stated, the general practice with our growers involves the cold frame method of plant growing and the following discussion considers only the best methods commonly employed here. As the plants develop, more water is needed and its application demands great care unless sub-irrigation is practiced. Mr. F. W. Mally, an extensive grower at Garrison, Texas, recommends five gallons a week as a rule for each of two lines of tile in a sub-irrigated 40-foot bed. In the cold frame as the plants grow larger more water may be needed toward the last.

As with the watering, ventilation of the bed and frame requires caution and watchfulness. At most times during bright days the sash should be slightly raised, or entirely removed, according to the temperature of the air. Even on dull days, unless too cold, every third sash should be raised a little at the bottom to allow some circulation of air. As the days grow warmer the sashes may be raised accordingly and before the final transplanting to the field the plants should be left uncovered nights as well as days.

FIELD SOIL.

The character of the field soil plays an important part in the early ripening of the tomato. The ideal soil is a warm light sandy loam, with a porous clay sub-soil. This responds readily to cultivation, and when lacking in plant food, manure and commercial fertilizers can be applied. Apply five or ten wagon loads of manure per acre about the middle of February, and after turning under, thoroughly pulverize the soil. On poor ground more manure may be used, but one must be careful not to get the soil too rich. Excessive fertility increases the amount of fruit, but retards and prolongs the period of ripening, hence, as earliness is an important requisite, quantity must be sacrificed for early maturity.

FERTILIZERS.

Tomatoes can hardly be successfully grown without fertilizers of some kind, and these must be applied at the right time in something like the right quantity. There are two general classes: barnyard and commercial.

BARNYARD MANURE.

Barnyard manure is the most generally used of all the different forms of fertilizers. There are many reasons for this; for instance, it is the most economical and easily obtained, and, besides containing plant food in the form of nitrogen, potash and phosphoric acid, it has a splendid physical effect on the soil. The greater part of the manure should be composted well and applied during the winter, early enough to become thoroughly incorporated in the soil before the opening of spring; or, it may be placed in piles and allowed to become well rotted, in which condition it may be applied to the land just before the plants are set.

COMMERCIAL FERTILIZERS.

Commercial fertilizers are being used more commonly every year, and they are becoming more and more essential to the successful growing of vegetables for the early market. Purchase the amount desired in early fall so that it will be on hand when needed. It is too expensive to be applied broadcast like manure, but should be worked in near the plant that it may be easily assimilated early in the season. Unless the soil is very poor, it is not necessary to apply over 250 pounds of muriate of potash, 200 pounds of acid phosphoric or ground bone and 100 pounds of nitrate of soda. These fertilizers should not be applied much in advance of the setting of the tomatoes on account of part of them being easily leached from the soil. The usefulness of commercial fertilizers as well as barnyard manure depends largely upon the condition of the land. Have the soil in a thorough state of cultivation and a small amount of fertilizer will do a vast amount of good.

Where the soil is ordinarily fertile excellent results have been obtained by small applications of nitrate of soda. As soon as the plants are established in the field the nitrate is sprinkled about the hill at the rate of 50 pounds per acre. Two weeks later a second application at the same rate is made and worked in along the sides of the rows. Nitrate of soda causes a steady, vigorous growth and from this reason tends to prevent "blossom drop," which is often caused by a sudden change from slow to rapid growing due to rain following a dry period.

TRANSPLANTING TO FIELD.

When the soil is warm, usually about the middle of March in East Texas, and the danger from frost is over, preparations may be made for removal of the plants from the cold frame to the field. On a bright, fair day strike off rows 3½ or 4 feet apart with a shovel plow, throwing out plenty of loose moist earth. While the rows are freshly laid off the plants should be brought on and set every 3 feet, firming them in well with an abundance of moist soil.

The plants are easily handled from bed to field in trays about 2½x3 feet loaded in a wagon bed. The trays are left at proper intervals along the rows, convenient for the planters who follow immediately after. To remove the plants from the bed to the trays first wet down the bed so that as much soil as possible will cling to the roots. Lift the plants with a flat mason's trowel, first cutting down each row space, and crosswise the bed also, with the sharp edge of the trowel so that a cube of earth will be taken up with each plant. The tomato is very tender with regard to its root system, and if this work is carelessly done the plants will recover slowly and a marked difference in earliness may result. Plants set during a dull cold day are likely to receive a severe check, the result of which will be manifest in blighted plants and late ripening fruits. The planters should be followed by a heel sweep or cultivator to fill the part of the trench not occupied by the plants and to level the field.

PRUNING, STAKING AND TYING.

From the time the plants reach the field until the fruit is gathered constant attention must be given to training and pruning. The single stem method has proven most profitable, from the fact that its use produces the earliest ripening, beside causing a uniformity in size that cannot be otherwise obtained. At setting time the lateral shoots which start from the axils of the leaves should be pinched out, and this operation must be frequently repeated during the season. Any sprouts or "suckers" from near the surface of the ground must be removed also, as well as any deformed or injured green fruit, thus keeping all the strength for the development of the single stem and the three good "hands" of fruit it will be allowed to maintain. When three well fruited clusters have established themselves, pinch off any others that form as well as the terminal bud itself.

Hand in hand with pruning goes the matter of staking and tying. The stakes should be prepared and ready at the time of setting. They may be anything from simple small straight poles cut from undergrowth to smooth, sawed 1-inch square lumber. The best stakes are stout, straight-grained material about 4 feet long. They must be placed so firmly in the ground that they will bear the weight of the plant and not "give" any under the strain of the strongest wind. As soon as the plants are fairly established in the field stakes should be put in and the plants tied. Raffia, such as is used in nurseries for tying in buds, is the most convenient tying material, but any common soft binding twine will do. Cut into convenient lengths and tie into hanks. To secure the plant to the stake wrap the cord once about the stem, cross lines and wrap twice about the stake. Draw snug and tie. In this manner the plant is held firm and close, yet not so as to choke or gall the stem. Two tyings will be required during the season and care should be taken that the ties are made in positions such as will support and protect the fruit as well as hold the stem.

CULTIVATION.

It matters little what variety of tomatoes is planted or how much fertilizer is used, if the land does not receive the proper amount and kind of tillage. If the land has been properly prepared, the cultivation during the growth of the plants, if done at the right time, will require very little labor.

RIDGE VERSUS LEVEL CULTURE.

During the last few years a great deal has been written upon ridge versus level culture. There are undoubtedly localities in Texas where the ridge method would be the best to use, while there are other localities in which level culture would give the best results. It depends largely upon the amount of rainfall and the nature of the soil. The results of experiments carried on by the different stations in regard to Irish potatoes are nearly all in favor of level culture. The advantage of this method is that it does not expose as much surface to the drying action of the sun and wind. Then, again, it is much easier to keep a surface mulch with level culture than when the ridge method is employed. The surface mulch, or dust blanket, is the best method for the retention of moisture, and, as the tomato requires large quantities of water for its best perfection, all means tending toward this end should be adopted. In soils that have an abundance or an excess of moisture throughout the growing season raised beds must be used, and to allow this the tomato rows should be 4½ feet apart. The plants may be set 2½ feet in the row. In the majority of places level culture will prove to be the more economical and will give better results than the ridge method. Each grower has a problem in the treatment of the conditions peculiar to his own land. No hard and fast rules can be given and each must use common sense in settling his own problem.

SHALLOW VERSUS DEEP CULTIVATION.

The only time the tomato land should receive deep cultivation is before the plants are set out. After that, if the land has been prepared properly, the soil need not be stirred more than 2 inches deep. The mistake is often made of laying by the tomato crop too soon. The soil should be cultivated until the fruit is ready for the first picking.

TOOLS.

One of the first steps a person should take who is going into the business of growing tomatoes is to buy himself a first-class set of tools. Every tomato grower should have a turning plow, five-toothed cultivator, and a disk or spring-toothed harrow, depending on the character of the soil. Weeds are very easily destroyed by the sweep, but it leaves a hard surface of the soil exposed from which moisture will escape in large quantities on a bright, windy day. The small cultivator will destroy weeds just as well, while at the same time it will leave a soil mulch that is of great service in preventing the escape of soil water.

INSECTS AND DISEASES.

From the time the seed vegetates until the fruit is gathered insect or fungus pests are constantly present, ready to take advantage of the weakness of the plant or the negligence of the grower. The intelligent and experienced planter has little to fear as he is familiar with these enemies, knows their traits and characteristics and has learned how to avoid, to prevent or to control them. The preparation of the hot bed by arranging for sub-irrigation and the wise selection of the field in reference to its drainage and its cut-worm history allows the plant to escape many of its most deadly foes. The placing of the trap crops and poisoned baits and the adoption of proper cultural methods will prevent, largely, injury which otherwise would prove serious. Those pests which cannot be avoided and for whose unwelcome visits there is no prevention can be controlled at least by thorough spraying methods.

The diseases most common are in order of their appearance: damping off, blight or leaf spot, wilt, blossom drop and fruit rot.

DAMPING OFF.

Damping off is caused by fungus diseases which are present in the soil, probably, at all times, but which are capable of doing most harm only in the presence of an excess of moisture and warmth, or in the absence of sunlight, or under some combination of these conditions. The plants decay at the surface of the ground or the stem wilts and the top falls.

By way of prevention have the soil rather light and the immediate surface of the bed dusted thoroughly with air slaked lime, sulphur, wood ashes, and tobacco dust. Leached ashes are first spread over the bed to a depth of an eighth of an inch, after which three parts air slaked lime and one part sulphur mixed are sifted lightly over the ashes. This is followed by a light coat of tobacco dust. Supply water to the bed by sub-irrigation if possible, and in any event avoid an excess of moisture (better too dry than too wet). Keep the frame well ventilated and the temperature steady at the degrees previously recommended. On dull days precautions must be redoubled. Plants in broadcast sown beds are especially liable to this disease and tomato seed should never be so planted.

LEAF SPOT.

The leaf spot or blight often starts in the cold frame, causing small discolored spots on the leaves. The diseased portions become more numerous and extensive in the field. The leaves turn yellow, and drop away. The plant goes from bad to worse until, finally, only the denuded stem is left. This is an easily recognized disease common to our tomato fields and generally distributed throughout East Texas. Treatment should be largely in the way of prevention. Strong, vigorous plants seem to withstand the disease to a considerable extent. While in the cold frame a thorough spray with Bordeaux mixture is usually desirable and two subsequent sprayings when in the field do much to assure healthy plants throughout the season. Diseased leaves should be burned, and, at the end of the season, all old vines should be destroyed in the same way.

TOMATO WILT.

The first intimation of the presence of this disease is the sudden wilting of the plant. The mysterious manner of attack and the feeling of helplessness experienced in the face of it causes the wilt especially to be dreaded by the grower. The disease, despite the awe it occasions, is not so serious as it seems, for though it "takes" and utterly destroys plants here and there, it rarely involves any considerable portion of the field, provided ordinary precautions are taken for its prevention.

The wilt is caused by bacteria, minute plants, which grow, multiply and flourish in the tissues of the tomato and so pack themselves into its cells that it becomes no longer possible for the sap to circulate freely, whereupon the leaf or plant collapses and the "wilt" results. The disease is spread from plant to plant largely by leaf eating insects. These pests after eating diseased tissues carry the germs on their jaws to healthy plants, thus disseminating the contagion. The remedy naturally suggests itself, simply poison the leaf eating insects. This is readily accomplished by adding four ounces of Paris green or two pounds of arsenate of lead to every fifty gallons of Bordeaux, when you spray for the leaf spot. As a further precaution wilted plants should be pulled up at once and burned, and at the end of the season the old plants should be destroyed by fire. In case the wilt has been troublesome tomatoes should not be planted on the same field the following year, it being supposed that the germ lives over in the soil. Avoid excessive nitrogen in the fertilizers used, as soft succulent plants are most easily affected by the disease.

BLOSSOM END ROT, OR BLACK ROT.

During a rainy season this is one of the most annoying fungus pests. It is especially disappointing to find at picking time a large per cent. of the crop ruined for market purposes by a small decayed spot on the otherwise perfect fruit. This spot usually appears at the blossom end of the fruit, but may occur at other places. The disease attacks the early fruit most seriously and is said to be induced by dry weather or excess of nitrogenous fertilizers. At the Troupe sub-station during the past season those plots which received potash and phosphoric acid only, and those which received no manure at all had the smallest per cent. of diseased fruit.

The measures usually recommended against the black rot are: use of hardy, stocky plants for setting, application of Bordeaux, as in the case of leaf spot, and destruction of diseased fruit by heat. Injured tomatoes should never be allowed to lie about on the ground, but should be gathered and thrown into a fire or buried in a deep pit.

Thorough cultivation tends to prevent black rot, as it is noticed that weeds and grass about the plant make the disease more serious. Tie so as to hold the fruit well from the ground.

BLOSSOM DROP.

Many people have been so discouraged from repeated failures due to the falling off of buds and blossoms that they have abandoned the tomato even for the kitchen garden. This trouble seems due to physiological causes rather than to any specific disease. Untoward weather conditions at blossoming time may cause the drop, owing

FIG. IV.
A Tomato Rot.
After Beach, N. Y. Agr. Exp. Station, Bul. 125.

to failure in pollenization. Any severe check to the growth of the plant, due to cold, drouth or excessive rain may bring about this disease. Too abundant nitrogenous manures is a fertile cause, and unpruned vines of luxuriant growth seem unable to hold their blossoms. In the way of prevention and remedy firm stocky plants to start with, constant cultivation and thorough pruning are recommended. Allow the plants for early market to set only three good hands of blossoms. If plants, cultivation and pruning are what they should be, these blossoms will have strength and vigor sufficient to set fruit unless especially unfortunate weather conditions prevail. Avoid heavy applications of nitrogen, and use more phosphate and potash.

Though it would seem that the tomato has its full share of trouble in the diseases, it still has a host of enemies, inasmuch that at no stage of growth is it without a possible insect pest. In the hot bed and cold frame it may be attacked by leaf miners and capsids, and in the field by cut-worms, tomato green-worms and boll worms.

THE LEAF MINER.

The serpentine leaf miner sometimes causes notable injury. This insect feeds on the tissue between the upper and lower epiderma of the leaf and is thus protected from both poisons and contact insecticides, hence treatment resolves itself into picking off and burning infected leaves. The injury is easily recognized as the mined channel turns and winds about in a characteristic manner. Whitish membranes formed by the upper and lower layer of dermal cells compose the roof and floor of the mine.

Injury from this insect seriously affected the growth of young plants in the college forcing house the past season.

TOMATO LEAF BUG.

A new tomato insect not hitherto recorded has caused serious injury at College Station. The State Entomologist, Mr. E. Dwight Sanderson, identifies the specimens handed him as *Dicyphus saparatus,* Uhl. This plant bug is a small, linear-form, dark-colored insect about one-eighth to three-sixteenths of an inch long. Larvæ, nymphs and adults fed on the under side of the leaf, causing it to curl and wither. They have long legs in comparison with the length and size of their bodies, and though the adults have good wings, they seldom use them.

If the bug appears in the hot bed or cold frame it can be readily controlled by smudging with tobacco stems at night. In the field if the plant is growing off vigorously it will probably take care of itself. In case these insects should prove too numerous and certain plants require treatment, a spray consisting of one pound of whale oil soap dissolved in four gallons of soft water applied so as to reach the under side of the leaves and thus cover the insects themselves will free the plant of these enemies. The insect moves sluggishly in the mornings, hence spraying should be done in the early part of the day.

CUT-WORMS.

The young of several species of moths are "cut-worms," and may prove very serious pests to the tomato grower. The moths lay their eggs on grass during spring and summer. The larvæ hatch a few weeks later and feed about on the grass, doing little noticeable injury that season. They are about half grown when approach of winter causes them to go into the ground for protection. If the grass is plowed under the following season, the cut-worms are deprived of their usual food. By the time the tomatoes are set out their appetite has a keen edge, and although they prefer fresh grass and clover, they are in a frame of mind to accept thankfully whatever comes to hand.

A lot of hungry cut-worms can soon destroy the fruits of two months' hard labor besides eliminating the prospect of an early crop, and it is essential that all means should be employed to prevent their presence. If the ground on which the tomatoes are to be planted is plowed early the previous summer and kept fallow throughout the season, the worms will be starved out and the soil will be free from them. However, in practice it is often difficult to arrange this program and another must be adopted. Deep plowing just before the worst weather sets in is often recommended, and though many worms may be destroyed by the weathering of the sod, a great many escape and the method proves but partially successful. Fortunately, the hungry worms come to poisoned baits readily, and by means of such traps the worm pest is most easily controlled. Plow and harrow the field a few weeks before time for transplanting, working the soil deep to aid in warming it. Poison a lot of clover, lambs quarter, pepper grass or mullein with a spray made by mixing a pound of Paris green or London purple in 100 gallons of water. Cut the clover or other poisoned plants, load on to a wagon and scatter over the tomato field in small bunches. This should be done a week before the time the tomatoes are brought to the field. This method will usually clear the patch of cut-worms if the bait has been thoroughly poisoned. Of course great care must be taken that no stock gets to the field, for if animals eat the baits death may follow.

In case some worms escape and cut plants are noticed, prepare wheat bran by mixing a teaspoonful of the above poisons with each quart, moisten and put a teaspoonful of this bait near each plant. These insects will leave tomatoes for bran every time. Cut-worm injury is done quickly, hence vigilance and quick action is essential on the part of the grower if he would save his plants.

A word in regard to natural enemies. Birds are especially fond of them, ground beetles, wasps and ants destroy great numbers, while the common garden toads devour them in wholesale quantities. As many as thirty-three cut-worms have been found in the stomach of a single toad.

THE BOLL WORM.

This boll worm is seldom troublesome on the early crop, especially if there is any early spring corn grown near the field, as the insect greatly prefers this food. In case tomatoes are found at picking time with the hole in the side indicating the presence of the worm, pick and crush or otherwise destroy it, that the worm may not survive. Professor Mally, in his recent report on the boll worm, fully discusses this insect. A copy of the report will be sent free on application.

THE TOMATO WORM.

This large green worm is well known to all planters. If the field is inspected regularly the worms will be seen before much damage is done. They are voracious feeders, however, and the field should be examined at least every other day after the first one is found. They are harmless to man in spite of their ferocious actions and grating of teeth when disturbed. Pick them off and crush or throw them into a can containing coal oil.

HARVESTING.

The first fruit to show signs of ripening requires longer to complete the process than those later in the season, and for this reason they should be allowed to take a good deal of color before being gathered. The later ones may be picked as soon as pink at the blossom end, for they ripen quickly on express trains and will be in good condition when they reach market. The field should be picked daily and care should be exercised to get everything at the proper degree of ripeness and none that are too green. It is the usual practice to remove the stem as soon as the fruit is picked.

For sorting and packing the tomatoes should be turned onto a smooth, clean table and carefully graded into two or more classes, according to the demands of your customers. The writer has known cases where five grades have been profitable, but for the present state of market for East Texas tomatoes three grades suffice for all practical purposes. In the fancy, nothing but smooth, perfect and even-sized and equally ripened tomatoes should be placed In No. 1 and No. 2 an equally careful classification should be maintained, and in no grade should inferior, rough or cracked fruit be allowed. It is to be borne in mind that the tomato is strictly for the fancy trade, and sells to those people who are able and willing to pay high prices. This trade does not want poor stuff at any price, hence anything less than a No. 1 will go unpurchased. The high-class restaurants will use No. 2 stock, but even this must be without serious blemish or deformity. It often proves unprofitable to ship a No. 2 fruit after the first part of the season. Dishonest packing brings retribution very quickly, and such packers are certain to lose money and reputation. To avoid the biased judgment one

FIG. V.
H. E. & W. T. R. R. Bulletin.
Scene on a Tomato Farm.

is almost certain to have regarding the quality of his own fruit, it is advisable to employ an experienced packer to grade your fruit. Do not feel hurt when you see him make No. 2 of what you feel sure should be No. 1. It is your eyes, and not the packer's that are at fault. In commercial practice the fruit is packed into three grades. Size and degree of ripeness are the main points. The packers select from the table a crate of "medium greens," those showing faint pink ends, of even size, then a crate of "half ripes," one-third red, and then a crate of "ripes," two-thirds red, always maintaining even size. . Nothing over two-thirds ripe should be packed, as it reaches market in bad condition. The field should be picked over daily. Nothing less than 2¼ inches in diameter is of value under ordinary conditions. In the best grade no more than six tomatoes should be necessary to fill the bottom layer of the basket. these should be laid stem end down. The upper layer in this grade may be larger, if of even size, to accommodate the flare of the basket. Twelve tomatoes may fill a basket, if large, and small toma-

FIG. VI.
H. E. & W. T. Ry. Bulletin.
Four Basket Crates in the Background.

toes should not be tucked in the top layer to fill corners. When more than fifteen are required to fill a basket, the fruit is too small. The top layer should have the stem ends up and outward, and the cover should press them firmly when nailed.

The crate should be neatly made of good stock and put together in a workmanlike manner. Misdriven nails, rough ends and untidy appearance lessen the market value of the goods no matter how excellent the quality of the fruit within. The common four basket crate is the package demanded by the market, and as this crate is in general use it can be readily obtained. There is something of a knack in packing the fruit in the baskets. The tomato must not be bruised or overcrowded, still they must be firmly in place and the basket fully and evenly filled. Practice and common sense will make an expert packer in a season. The experienced master of the packing table can tell the degree of ripeness of fruit at a glance, and classifies with this in mind as well as evenness of size and degree of blemish. He discovers the overgrown and the too deformed fruit at once, and sends a warning to the careless picker. Upon the care, neatness and perfection of his work depend the financial success of this enterprise, and the market reputation of the planter. The crate should be plainly marked on both ends with the name and address of the shipper, or his number, and the name of the party to whom his stock is sent, unless carload shipments are being made.

From the time the tomato leaves the field until it reaches the consumer there should be no delay. The fruit should be handled as carefully and as seldom as possible. Rough pickers and sorters may make bruises which do not show at all from the shipper's end, but may appear as soft spots in time to ruin the sale of the stock. The long ride in a close express car brings out all the blemishes or bruises as rapidly as it ripens the fruit. The iced freight is the most satisfactory method of shipping, as it allows longer time on the vine, and this gives the better quality due to a degree more of natural ripening.

MARKETING.

The problem of marketing deserves more discussion than the nature of this bulletin will allow, hence only short statements will be made setting forth various methods.

Method 1. Consignment to Commission Firms.

This method requires the least brain work and the least effort on the part of the grower. He sends his product to the commission man, who sells it on the open market and returns to the grower the proceeds, less express, drayage and 10 per cent. commission charges. This appears fair and satisfactory on the face of it, but in practice the method is highly unsatisfactory. In the first place, it is difficult to find a commission firm that will work largely in the interest of the grower, in fact, there is no evidence to show that such a firm has ever existed, while, secondly, it often occurs that the firm to which one consigns is dishonest, and small returns, or none at all, are made to the shipper. There is no way to determine the honest from the dishonest. Their standing at their bank or in commercial reviews shows nothing as to the honor of their business transactions, nor does it guarantee that they look out for the grower's interests. From long dealings with commission firms one is led to suspect that first of all they are after their 10 per cent. and such profits as may be had from drayage charges; secondly, they are working to hold customers and to retain their patronage, and, lastly, they are striving to keep the grower sending on more truck. Their chief interests are antagonistic to those of the grower, which, as a consequence, suffer.

As said above, this method is the easiest for the planter. You address the shipment and bid it farewell at the station, or, figuratively, you simply shut your eyes and let go, never knowing where you will land until the bump occurs. Though simple and easy, it is hardly to be advised.

Method 2. Selling at Track.

This method is more troublesome than the first named, but is more satisfactory. It involves neighborhood co-operation, as it will be necessary to have sufficient quantities for sale to warrant several buyers in visiting your town. A local trucker's association should be formed and the secretary required to get into communication with buyers before the crop comes on, notifying them when the first picking will be ready and what amounts of truck are likely to be for sale. This enables the buyers to plan ahead and be on hand when the crop begins to ripen.

There are weak points in plan No. 2, for the side track prices range lower than the northern market by an amount sufficient to cover freight and express, drayage, commission, expense and wages of buyer and risk of purchasing perishable goods. This lower range of prices discourages individuals who perhaps are receiving alluring quotations from commission merchants. These individuals revert to method No. 1, and the buyers, unable to purchase in quantities and discouraged by seeing consignments sent out, leave the town. Thus in the midst of the season co-operation ceases, there is a general reversion to method No. 1, and loss and discouragement follow. Method No. 2, properly fortified and modified, may prove very satisfactory, however. The association should have a strong centralized government, and the members should be bound to deliver their truck to their duly appointed officers. These officers should have entire charge of the sales, and should be placed under bond or their honesty insured. In addition to these provisions, another officer properly bonded or insured, and on salary, should be stationed at some principal market to sell stock, inspect shipments and keep the association officers at home posted daily on the markets. In this manner the buyers have to pay the market price less freight only, or the truck is sold by the representative at the other end.

When shipments amount to several cars a day this representative must be a man of exceptional business ability to successfully handle those cars which the buyers fail to purchase at track. This method has proven very profitable at several places, and is the most satisfactory plan known to the writer for local communities.

The following quotations are from the secretary of the Mt. Selman Tomato Co., written in reply to specific questions as to how that company disposed of the tomato crop:

"Replying to yours of the 17th, will say that a good strong association should have a man in the Northern or Eastern market to keep them posted in regard to the conditions of the market daily. We had a man in Chicago this season, but we secured better results from Eastern markets. The Eastern buyers have turned their attention to this country, and no doubt we will get better results from the East in the coming season.

"We make ourselves known to all the different markets and all the different buyers so that when the season opens we have no trouble to find a buyer for our stuff.

"We do not depend on any one market. We keep posted as nearly as possible with all the different markets, and do our own business. We give no middle man 3 or 5 per cent. to do it for us. Hoping this will give you an idea as to how we do business, I remain,   "Yours truly,
                                        "R. V. DUBLIN, Secretary."

Method 3.   Contract Sale.

A plan sometimes adopted by very young and inexperienced truckers' associations is that of contracting the season's crop at a stated price. The contract purchaser takes everything very readily while the market price equals or exceeds the contract price, but finds the stock "injured and not up to grade" as soon as the market falls below the price agreed on. Expensive litigation with doubtful outcome confronts the grower, and rather than take the chances the loss is shouldered.

Method 4.   Exchange.

The final outcome of the marketing problem probably will be the complete organization of an exchange, similar to that of California. This simply means the extension of method No. 2 to cover the requirements of the State instead of the community. It of necessity will require men of great executive ability for officers and a high standard of intelligence, confidence and socialistic sentiment among the rank and file. It is possible that these men and conditions will be found quickly, and such is earnestly hoped, but it is more likely that a few years will elapse before the exchange system will be perfected. Meanwhile, method No. 2 is the one to be recommended; method No. 1 to be used if necessary, and method No. 3 to be studiously avoided, and method No. 4 to be worked for by all interested in the welfare of the truckers of the State.

CONCLUSION.

How much will it cost to produce an acre of tomatoes, what number of crates of marketable fruit does an acre produce, and what is the price per crate usually obtained by the grower? These are questions often asked by beginners, and the replies here given are by conservative and successful East Texas growers. The total cost of an acre of tomatoes is from $40.00 to $60.00, the range of yield from 75 to 200 crates, while prices vary from 40 to 90 cents per crate. These replies are based on experience in 1902. Small plantations carefully tended usually produce the largest crop and net the greatest profits per acre. Fifty acres, at least, are necessary that carload shipments may be made.

The question of over-production is often discussed at truckers' associations, and the concensus of opinion is that there is no danger of this if adequate means of distribution are found? A properly conducted "exchange" would provide this, placing shipments, rightly proportioned, in every city in the North, and under such systematized marketing it is not probable that the supply would ever meet the demand.

ED. J. KYLE.
EDWARD C. GREEN.

Printed in Great
Britain
by Amazon